PROPHECY *in* CONTEXT

A LOOK AT THE OLIVET DISCOURSE

BOB SHELTON

JOURNEYFORTH

Greenville, South Carolina

Library of Congress Cataloging-in-Publication Data

Shelton, Bob, 1929-
  Prophecy in context / Bob Shelton.
     p. cm.
  Includes bibliographical references (p.   ).
  Summary: "This book is a detailed study of Christ's Olivet
Discourse from Matthew 24–25"—Provided by publisher.
  ISBN 978-1-59166-851-0 (perfect bound pbk. : alk. paper)
  1. Bible. N.T. Matthew XIV-XXV—Commentaries. 2. End
of the world. I. Title.
  BS2575.6.E7S54 2008
  226.2'06—dc22

                                            2008003842

Cover Photo Credits: © 2008 iStockphoto Inc.

All Scripture is quoted from the Authorized King James
Version.

Prophecy in Context

Design by Nick Ng
Page layout by Michael Boone

© 2008 by BJU Press
Greenville, South Carolina 29614
JourneyForth Books is a division of BJU Press

Printed in the United States of America

ISBN 978-1-59166-851-0

15 14 13 12 11 10 9 8 7 6 5 4 3 2 1

My wife, Nancy, and I dedicate this book to our children, Becky, Shari, and Dan. Their faithful walk with Christ has been a great encouragement to us and our ministry.

CONTENTS

FOREWORD

Born-again Christians take note! The day of our glorification in Christ—by means of the Rapture—is drawing ever closer. It is therefore absolutely urgent that we cling to every word God has written concerning the end of this age.

My friend Bob Shelton has made a fine contribution to our understanding of "The Olivet Discourse" of our Lord Jesus Christ in Matthew 24 and 25. He carefully and clearly outlines what our Lord taught us concerning the Great Tribulation, the signs of His coming, and the destiny of the true church and of ethnic Israel.

Many today are denying that the church will escape the horrors of the Tribulation. Others teach that most of what Christ taught about these events happened in AD 70! More than ever, God's people need to "search the scriptures daily to find out whether these things are so" (Acts 17:11). My prayer is that this book will be used of God to help many to understand "the times and the seasons" of Bible prophecy.

John C. Whitcomb

Preface

Someone has well said, "A text out of context is a pretext." I don't know of any portion of Scripture that has been lifted out of context more often than Matthew 24–25. As the result of this many reach conclusions that do not fit God's prophetic plan. For example, many have declared one or more of the following:

- "The signs of Matthew 24 must take place before the Rapture."
- "Those 'taken' in the 'two in the field' passage in Matthew 24:40 are believers who are caught up in the Rapture while those who are 'left' are unsaved who will enter tribulation days on earth."
- "The wise and foolish virgins of Matthew 25:1–2 represent believers and unbelievers at the time of the rapture."
- "The sheep and the goats of Matthew 25:32 are good and bad nations."

Let me say it as gently as I know how. I don't believe any of these statements. On the pages that follow you will discover why. Matthew 24–25 contain the teachings of Christ during His Olivet Discourse. He presented great prophetic truths, but they are valid only when they are left in context.

Acknowledgments

To my beloved wife for her diligent work in typing the original manuscript.

To Jean Martin for her expertise in grammar and punctuation.

To the faithful people of BJU Press for their efforts in preparing and printing this book, with special thanks to Suzette Jordan for her keen insight and wise counsel.

1

"WHEN SHALL THESE THINGS BE?"

And Jesus went out, and departed from the temple: and his disciples came to him for to shew him the buildings of the temple. And Jesus said unto them, See ye not all these things? verily I say unto you, There shall not be left here one stone upon another, that shall not be thrown down. And as he sat upon the mount of Olives, the disciples came unto him privately, saying, Tell us, when shall these things be? (Matt. 24:1–3a)

The Olivet Discourse has long been the subject of much study and debate. As we look at it again, we need to keep the prophetic events of this passage in context. There are those who believe that the events Jesus spoke of in Matthew 24–25 must occur before the Rapture. The truth is they will follow the Rapture but will occur before the millennial kingdom.

When the disciples asked Jesus, "What shall be the sign of thy coming?" (Matt. 24:3), they were not asking for signs that must occur before His coming to rapture the church. When they asked the question, the church did not exist. They were looking for His coming to set up His kingdom. In His Olivet Discourse Jesus answered their question.

One of the many titles of the Lord Jesus is "Prophet." During His time with the disciples He had prophesied many things concerning Himself.

He Prophesied His Betrayal

Jesus and His disciples had gathered in Jerusalem in the Upper Room for their last Passover meal together.

> And as they did eat, he said, Verily I say unto you, that one of you shall betray me. And they were exceeding sorrowful, and began every one of them to say unto him, Lord, is it I? And he answered and said, He that dippeth his hand with me in the dish, the same shall betray me. The Son of man goeth as it is written of him: but woe unto that man by whom the Son of man is betrayed! it had been good for that man if he had not been born. Then Judas, which betrayed him, answered and said, Master, is it I? He said unto him, Thou hast said. (Matt. 26:21–25)

He Prophesied His Death

When Jesus was in Bethany, in the house of Simon the leper, Mary, the sister of Martha and Lazarus, came to Him with

> an alabaster box of very precious ointment, and poured it on his head, as he sat at meat. But when his disciples saw it, they had indignation, saying, To what purpose is this waste? For this ointment might have been sold for much, and given to the poor. When Jesus understood it, he said unto them, Why trouble ye the woman? for

she hath wrought a good work upon me. For ye have
the poor always with you; but me ye have not always.
For in that she hath poured this ointment on my body,
she did it for my burial. (Matt. 26:6–12)

He Prophesied His Resurrection

Following the Lord's purification of the temple,

the Jews . . . said unto him, What sign shewest thou unto
us, seeing that thou doest these things? Jesus answered
and said unto them, Destroy this temple, and in three
days I will raise it up. Then said the Jews, Forty and six
years was this temple in building, and wilt thou rear it
up in three days? But he spake of the temple of his body.
When therefore he was risen from the dead, his disciples
remembered that he had said this unto them; and they
believed the scripture, and the word which Jesus had
said. (John 2:18–22)

He Prophesied His Coming for His Bride

The first time Jesus spoke of the rapture of the church
He declared, "In my Father's house are many mansions:
if it were not so, I would have told you. I go to prepare
a place for you. And if I go and prepare a place for you, I
will come again, and receive you unto myself; that where
I am, there ye may be also" (John 14:2–3).

He Prophesied His Return to the Earth

During the Olivet Discourse the Lord prophesied His
return: "When the Son of man shall come in his glory,
and all the holy angels with him, then shall he sit upon
the throne of his glory" (Matt. 25:31).

As we return to our text in Matthew 24, we discover that Jesus also prophesied the coming destruction of the temple. The response of the disciples was "When shall these things be?" Jesus could have said, "In thirty-seven years a general by the name of Titus, the son of Vespasian, will enter the city of Jerusalem with his mighty Roman army. Thousands of Jews will be led to the Mount of Olives, where they will be crucified. Hundreds of thousands of men, women, and children will be slaughtered in the streets of Jerusalem." He could have answered their question with facts and dates, but He didn't. He told them all they needed to know. Perhaps there is a lesson here for modern prognosticators who are forever setting dates for special events on God's prophetic calendar.

Harold Camping wrote over five hundred pages in his book *1994?* to present his conviction that "1994 looks more and more like a candidate for the year of Christ's return."[1]

Edgar C. Whisenant wrote *The Rapture: Rosh Hash Ana, 1988, and 88 Reasons Why*, which he begins by saying, "You only need one good solid reason why 1988 will be the church's Rapture. Here are 88 reasons why 1988 looks like the year of the church's rapture."[2] I was not surprised to read Mr. Whisenant's next book *The Final Shout: Rapture Report 1989* and to discover that chapter 1 bears this heading: "What Went Wrong in 1988—and Why?"[3]

Students of Bible prophecy must be careful lest they make predictions that are not in line with God's prophetic Word.

2

"THE SIGN OF THY COMING"

And as he sat upon the mount of Olives, the disciples came unto him privately, saying, Tell us, when shall these things be? and what shall be the sign of thy coming, *and of the end of the world? (Matt. 24:3)*

.

After Jesus had made His prophetic announcement, the first question from the disciples was "When shall these things be?" That is, "When will the temple be destroyed?" Christ had told them all they needed to know, so their question regarding the timing of the destruction went unanswered.

They moved on to their next question: "What shall be the sign of thy coming?" If John Kerr's timetable is correct in *A Harmony of the Gospels*, the disciples asked the question on Tuesday of the Passion Week. Two days later Jesus shared with them the prophecy of His coming to receive His bride unto Himself: "In my Father's house are many mansions: if it were not so, I would have told you. I go to prepare a place for you. And if I go and prepare a place for you, I will come again, and receive you unto myself; that where I am, there ye may be also" (John 14:2–3). When the disciples asked, "What shall be the sign of thy coming," they had not yet been told of the coming of Christ to rapture the church.[1]

It is my conviction that the Rapture is not spoken of in the Old Testament nor found in the Synoptic Gospels (Matthew, Mark, and Luke). The Old Testament and the Synoptics have many references to our Lord's return to the earth to set up His kingdom, but the first mention of the Rapture was from the lips of Christ recorded in John 14:2–3. Even then, when He mentioned it, He didn't give much information on the subject. For that reason when the Holy Spirit inspired Paul to write about the Rapture, he began by saying, "Behold I shew you a mystery" (1 Cor. 15:51). The Rapture was a mystery to the church at Corinth because they didn't know much about it.

When the disciples asked for a sign, they knew nothing of His return to rapture the church. The coming of Christ to them meant His coming to set up an earthly kingdom.

They had already been arguing over who would be the greatest in the kingdom. The mother of James and John had asked the Lord to grant that her two sons might sit in positions of authority, one on His right hand and the other on His left in His kingdom (Matt. 20:21).

James and John themselves later made the same request:

And James and John, the sons of Zebedee, come unto him, saying, Master, we would that thou shouldest do for us whatsoever we shall desire. And he said unto them, What would ye that I should do for you? They said unto him, Grant unto us that we may sit, one on thy right hand, and the other on thy left hand, in thy glory. (Mark 10:35–37)

Because the disciples knew the truth of Isaiah 1:26— "I will restore thy judges as at the first"—when they heard Christ say, "Ye also shall sit upon twelve thrones, judging the twelve tribes of Israel" (Matt. 19:28), they were certain that the day would come when Christ would rule over Israel and that He would use them as judges in His theocracy.

When they asked for signs, Jesus answered their question by giving them many events that will occur before His return to earth to set up His kingdom. There are no signs that must be fulfilled before Christ comes to catch His bride away, but many signs will be fulfilled before His revelation.

John Walvoord and Roy Zuck wrote,

These two questions prompted the following discussion by Jesus, commonly called the Olivet discourse (Matt. 24–25). The questions related to the destruction of the temple and Jerusalem, and the sign of the Lord's coming and the end of the age. They have nothing to do with the church, which Jesus said He would build (16:18). The church is not present in any sense in chapters 24 and 25.[2]

We will look at Jesus' answers in the next chapter.

3

"THE BEGINNING OF SORROWS"

And Jesus answered and said unto them, Take heed that no man deceive you. For many shall come in my name, saying, I am Christ; and shall deceive many. And ye shall hear of wars and rumours of wars: see that ye be not troubled: for all these things must come to pass, but the end is not yet. For nation shall rise against nation, and kingdom against kingdom: and there shall be famines, and pestilences, and earthquakes, in divers places. All these are the beginning of sorrows. (Matt. 24:4–8)

There are those who teach that the signs spoken of in these verses must take place before Christ comes for His bride. The fact is, many of these disturbances are happening now, but they are not precursors of the Rapture. If the events of Matthew 24 must occur before the Rapture, then the Rapture is not imminent. Dwight Pentecost writes, "The doctrine of imminence forbids the participation of the church in any part of the seventieth week."[1] The events of Matthew 24 will take place before His second coming—also called the Revelation of Christ. To grasp this truth, we must have a clear understanding of the order of events on God's prophetic timetable.

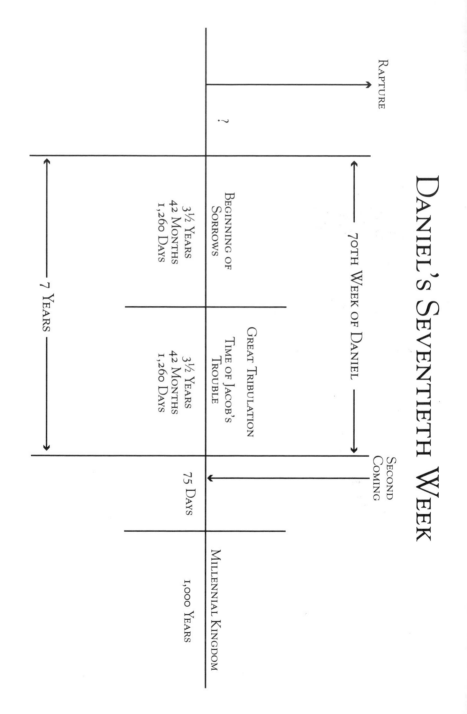

Daniel's Seventieth Week

Rapture

?

70th Week of Daniel

Beginning of Sorrows
3½ Years
42 Months
1,260 Days

Great Tribulation
Time of Jacob's Trouble
3½ Years
42 Months
1,260 Days

7 Years

Second Coming

75 Days

Millennial Kingdom
1,000 Years

Note that there will be a gap of time between the Rapture and the beginning of a seven-year period called the Seventieth Week. We don't know how long that gap will be, but it must be long enough for the Antichrist to rise up out of the Revived Roman Empire referred to in Daniel 7:7—"After this I saw in the night visions, and behold a fourth beast, dreadful and terrible, and strong exceedingly; and it had great iron teeth: it devoured and brake in pieces, and stamped the residue with the feet of it: and it was diverse from all the beasts that were before it; and it had ten horns."

The fourth beast Daniel saw in the vision he received from God is the same as the iron legs Nebuchadnezzar saw in the dream he received from God (Dan. 2:33*a*). The fourth beast and the iron legs represented the Old Roman Empire. That empire died in 476 AD, but the day is coming when ten nations will unite over the ashes of the Old Roman Empire and form the Revived Roman Empire. Nebuchadnezzar saw it in the form of ten toes (Dan. 2:42). Daniel saw it in the form of ten horns (Dan. 7:7). H. A. Ironside speaks of this in his book *Daniel*:

> This brings us to the last form of the fourth kingdom; for the Roman empire, though at present in abeyance, has not yet come to its end. The ten toes on the feet of the image represent ten kings who are to reign at one time, but who will form a confederacy on the ground of the ancient empire. This is something which the world has never yet seen.[2]

Daniel's prophecy continues in 7:8—"I considered the horns, and, behold, there came up among them another little horn, before whom there were three of the first horns plucked up by the roots: and, behold, in

11

this horn were eyes like the eyes of man, and a mouth speaking great things."

The "little horn" is one of twenty-six names or titles of the Antichrist. He is identified as a man with "a mouth speaking great things." It is the exact terminology of Revelation 13:4*b*–5*a*. "Who is like unto the beast? who is able to make war with him? And there was given unto him a mouth speaking great things."

Seven of the ten nations will acquiesce to the control of Antichrist while the other three will be brought into the union by force. They will be "horns plucked up by the roots" (Dan. 7:8). He will then have the military muscle to guarantee the peace of Israel for seven years (Dan. 9:27). When he signs that covenant, the Seventieth Week will begin.

We know from Scripture that the Seventieth Week will be exactly seven years (2520 days on the Jewish calendar). During those days the horrible judgments of the book of Revelation will take place. These judgments are divided into three groupings: seals, trumpets and vials. The first four of the seal judgments are found in Revelation 6:1–8. They are referred to as the four horsemen of the Apocalypse. Note how they parallel the events of Matthew 24:5–7:

Matthew 24	Revelation 6
Vs. 5—Hunger for a global leader who will declare himself to be the Christ	Vs. 2—Such a man will appear on a white horse

Vs. 6—Wars and rumors of wars	Vs. 4—Second horseman will appear on a red horse and take "peace from the earth"
Vs. 7*a*—Famines	Vs. 6—Rider of the black horse brings unbelievable famine to the earth
Vs. 7*b*—Pestilences and earthquakes	Vs. 8—Rider of the pale horse will bring such destruction that one-fourth of earth's population will die

This period is further identified in Matthew 24:8: "All these are the beginning of sorrows." Most Bible commentators refer to the first half of the Seventieth Week as the "Beginning of Sorrows." The second three-and-a-half years are referred to as the "Great Tribulation," or the "Time of Jacob's Trouble."

4

"Endure unto the End"

Then shall they deliver you up to be afflicted, and shall kill you: and ye shall be hated of all nations for my name's sake. And then shall many be offended, and shall betray one another, and shall hate one another. And many false prophets shall rise, and shall deceive many. And because iniquity shall abound, the love of many shall wax cold. But he that shall endure unto the end, the same shall be saved. (Matt. 24:9–13)

I have already noted that Matthew 24:5–8 corresponds to Revelation 6:1–8. These verses, in both texts, speak of events during the first half of the Seventieth Week, the "Beginning of Sorrows." In both texts the following verses introduce the "Great Tribulation."

Matthew 24:9	Revelation 6:9
"Then shall they deliver you up to be afflicted, and shall kill you: and ye shall be hated of all nations for my name's sake."	"And when he had opened the fifth seal, I saw under the altar the souls of them that were slain for the word of God, and for the testimony which they held."

In both accounts the scene changes from the "Beginning of Sorrows" to the "Great Tribulation." And what tribulation there shall be! Tribulation saints will be hated, afflicted, and murdered. Even among the unsaved there will be betrayal, hate, and abounding iniquity. Little wonder Jesus went on to say, "But he that shall endure unto the end, the same shall be saved" (Matt. 24:13). Christ is not speaking of soul salvation. A person is not saved by endurance; he is saved by the cleansing blood of God's crucified Lamb. The salvation in verse 13 is the salvation of mortal bodies as people flee and hide from the awful wrath that will come on all the earth.

Jesus goes on in verse 22 to say, "Except those days should be shortened [terminated], there should no flesh be saved." Notice that He is speaking of salvation of the flesh. It is easy to understand what Jesus meant when we read the tally of death from the seal, trumpet, and vial judgments. It appears at least three-fourths of all the people on earth will be dead by the end of the Seventieth Week. If those days were not terminated, no one would survive (Matt. 24:22).

5

"GOSPEL OF THE KINGDOM"

And this gospel of the kingdom *shall be preached in all the world for a witness unto all nations; and then shall the end come. (Matt. 24:14)*

In the midst of all the death and heartache of the Seventieth Week a marvelous thing will happen—the gospel of the kingdom shall be preached. This is the same gospel we preach today. It is called "the gospel of the kingdom" because it will be preached just prior to the kingdom.

I regularly do a national radio program and once received a letter from a listener who said, "If the Rapture had already happened, there would not be any preachers left to preach the gospel." Oh, but there will be preachers. First, the gospel will be preached by Elijah and Moses. We read of their witness for 1260 days (the first half of the Seventieth Week) in Revelation 11:3–6:

> And I will give power unto my two witnesses, and they
> shall prophesy a thousand two hundred and threescore
> days, clothed in sackcloth. These are the two olive trees,
> and the two candlesticks standing before the God of the
> earth. And if any man will hurt them, fire proceedeth
> out of their mouth, and devoureth their enemies: and
> if any man will hurt them, he must in this manner be
> killed. These have power to shut heaven, that it rain
> not in the days of their prophecy: and have power over
> waters to turn them to blood, and to smite the earth
> with all plagues, as often as they will.

From the description of their actions, under God's authority and power, they are clearly identified as Elijah and Moses. The gospel will also be presented by 144,000 Jewish men. The account of their conversion is recorded in Revelation 7:4–8. They are called "the first fruits unto God and the Lamb" (Rev. 14:4*b*).

The question often arises of how can Elijah and Moses preach and the 144,000 witness without the Holy Spirit. This question comes from a misunderstanding of 2 Thessalonians 2:7, which says, "For the mystery of iniquity doth already work: only he who now letteth will let, until he be taken out of the way."

People tend to conclude that at the time of the Rapture the Holy Spirit will be taken to heaven and stay there. That cannot be. The Holy Spirit will be removed in the sense that He abides in the bodies of all who have trusted Christ as Savior, but the emphasis in verse 7 is His restraining influence on the earth through the church.

The church will be removed at the Rapture, but the Holy Spirit will remain on earth to continue His work in bringing people to Christ. Dwight Pentecost has it correct when he writes, "The Holy Spirit does not cease His ministries with the removal of the church, nor does He cease to be omnipresent . . . but the restraining ministry does cease."[1]

At the time of the Rapture there will not be one believer left on earth. There is no such thing as a partial or split rapture. All who know Christ as Savior will be caught up to meet the Lord in the air: "Then we which are alive and remain shall be caught up together with them in the clouds to meet the Lord in the air: and so shall we ever be with the Lord" (1 Thess. 4:17).

No longer will the church be under the command of Christ to "preach the gospel to every creature," but the Holy Spirit will use His Word through the preaching of Elijah and Moses and the witness of the 144,000 Jewish evangelists. As a result, multitudes will come to Christ as Savior.

The intimate relationship with the Holy Spirit enjoyed by church-age saints will not be the experience of tribulation saints. In John 14:17 Jesus said to the apostles, "He [the Holy Spirit] dwelleth with you, and shall be in you." Though there were times when the Holy Spirit entered the bodies of Old Testament saints to accomplish a special work, it could not be said that their bodies were the "temples of the Holy Spirit." He was with them but not abiding in them.

Likewise, the Holy Spirit, who is in the bodies of believers during the church age, will be with tribulation saints. Dwight Pentecost expresses this truth in these words: "In the tribulation period, the Holy Spirit, who is omnipresent, will do the work of regeneration as He did when God was previously dealing with Israel, but without an indwelling ministry."[2]

Jesus clearly stated, "He dwelleth with you, and shall be in you" (John 14:17). Today we can say He dwells in us, church-age saints, and shall be with them, tribulation saints. He will be doing His work then as He is working now to draw people to Jesus Christ.

We know the Holy Spirit will be on earth during tribulation days because His ministry is presented in the Olivet Discourse. Our Lord's discourse is recorded not only in Matthew 24–25 but also in Mark 13 and Luke 21. It is in Mark's account that we read, "But when they shall lead you, and deliver you up, take no thought beforehand what ye shall speak, neither do ye premeditate: but whatsoever shall be given you in that hour, that speak ye: for it is not ye that speak, but the Holy Ghost" (Mark 13:11).

As a result of Moses' and Elijah's Holy Spirit–empowered preaching of the gospel for 1260 days, Antichrist will have them killed. It will be the first time for Elijah to taste of physical death, while Moses, like several others in Scripture, will die the second time. These dramatic events are recorded in Revelation 11:7–12:

> And when they shall have finished their testimony, the beast that ascendeth out of the bottomless pit shall make war against them, and shall overcome them, and kill them. And their dead bodies shall lie in the street of the great city, which spiritually is called Sodom and Egypt, where also our Lord was crucified. And they of the people and kindreds and tongues and nations shall see their dead bodies three days and an half, and shall not suffer their dead bodies to be put in graves. And

they that dwell upon the earth shall rejoice over them, and make merry, and shall send gifts one to another; because these two prophets tormented them that dwelt on the earth. And after three days and an half the Spirit of life from God entered into them, and they stood upon their feet; and great fear fell upon them which saw them. And they heard a great voice from heaven saying unto them, Come up hither. And they ascended up to heaven in a cloud; and their enemies beheld them.

Yes, I believe in a midtribulation rapture, but it is for only two men—not for the church. Another great development will take place in the middle of the Seventieth Week, as we will see in the next chapter.

6

"GREAT TRIBULATION"

When ye therefore shall see the abomination of desolation, spoken of by Daniel the prophet, stand in the holy place (whoso readeth, let him understand): then let them which be in Judaea flee into the mountains: let him which is on the housetop not come down to take any thing out of his house: neither let him which is in the field return back to take his clothes. And woe unto them that are with child, and to them that give suck in those days! But pray ye that your flight be not in the winter, neither on the sabbath day: for then shall be great tribulation, such as was not since the beginning of the world to this time, no, nor ever shall be. (Matt. 24:15–21)

Daniel 9 is a vital piece of this prophetic puzzle. There we read, "And he shall confirm the covenant with many for one week: and in the midst of the week he shall cause the sacrifice and the oblation to cease, and for the overspreading of abominations he shall make it desolate" (Dan. 9:27).

This verse not only tells us when the Seventieth Week begins but also tells us when the "great tribulation" will start. As we noted earlier, the Seventieth Week will begin when Antichrist signs a covenant guaranteeing the peace of Israel for seven years.

DANIEL'S SEVENTY WEEKS

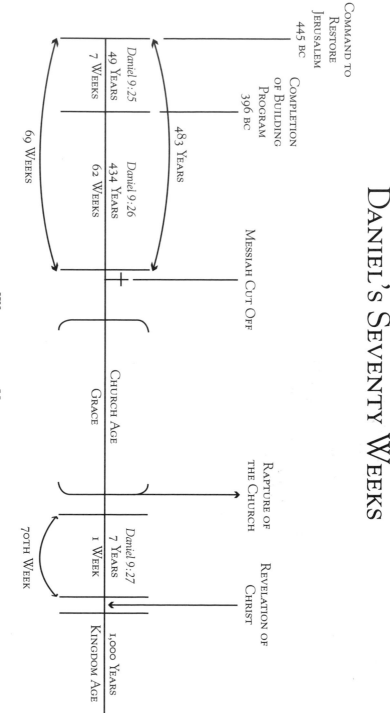

COMMAND TO
RESTORE
JERUSALEM
445 BC

COMPLETION
OF BUILDING
PROGRAM
396 BC

Daniel 9:25
49 YEARS
7 WEEKS

Daniel 9:26
434 YEARS
62 WEEKS

483 YEARS

69 WEEKS

MESSIAH CUT OFF

CHURCH AGE
GRACE

RAPTURE OF
THE CHURCH

REVELATION OF
CHRIST

Daniel 9:27
7 YEARS
1 WEEK

70TH WEEK

1,000 YEARS
KINGDOM AGE

70 WEEKS = 490 YEARS

We know this treaty has to do with Israel, for the Seventieth Week, as well as the other sixty-nine weeks (483 years), deals with God's prophetic plan for Israel. In Daniel 9:24 we read, "Seventy weeks are determined upon thy people." Daniel's people were the Jews.

"And in the midst of the week he shall cause the sacrifice and the oblation to cease, and for the overspreading of abominations he shall make it desolate" (Dan. 9:27). The Hebrew word for *week* is *shabua*. It simply means seven. Since the Seventieth Week is seven years, the "midst of the week" has reference to three and a half years from its beginning. In other words, the first half of the Seventieth Week will be three and a half years (42 months, or 1260 days), and the second half will be three and a half years (42 months, or 1260 days).

What marks the arrival of the midway point? "And in the midst of the week he shall cause the sacrifice and the oblation to cease, and for the overspreading of abominations he shall make it desolate" (Dan. 9:27). Antichrist will not only break his covenant with Israel, he will also set up an image like himself in the temple and demand that the whole world bow down to worship his image (Rev. 13:13–15). This is "the abomination of desolation" Jesus spoke of in our text. "When ye therefore shall see the abomination of desolation, spoken of by Daniel the prophet, stand in the holy place" (Matt. 24:15).

The eyes of millions of Jews will open. They will believe the message they have been hearing from Elijah and Moses for three and a half years as well as the faithful witness of the 144,000.

It will be clear to them that the world leader whom they have embraced as their messiah is the Antichrist.

They will reject the mark he will impose on all who bow the knee to him (Rev. 13:16–17). They will also refuse to bow before his image, for both receiving the mark and bowing down to the image are forbidden in Scripture. Concerning the mark, "Ye shall not make any cuttings in your flesh for the dead, nor print any marks upon you" (Lev. 19:28). Concerning the image, "Thou shalt have no other gods before me. Thou shalt not make unto thee any graven image, or any likeness of any thing that is in heaven above, or that is in the earth beneath, or that is in the water under the earth: thou shalt not bow down thyself to them, nor serve them" (Exod. 20:3–5*a*). Believing Jews will then "flee into the mountains" (Matt. 24:16), but no doubt millions will flee into all the world. The days that follow are referred to by Jesus as the "great tribulation" (Matt. 24:21). As they go, they will be sharing the gospel story with Gentiles, resulting in the conversion of millions. These uprooted Jewish believers will be God's great missionary society to be "a witness unto all nations; and then shall the end come" (Matt. 24:14). This is not the church involved in the Great Commission, but it is believing Israel witnessing to all the world—then the end of the Great Tribulation will come.

The three Hebrew young men who were cast into Nebuchadnezzar's fiery furnace present a perfect Old Testament picture of displaced believing Jews during tribulation days. The Scofield Reference Bible footnote of this story in Daniel 3 reads, "The three Jews, faithful to God while the nation of Israel far from their land bear no testimony, are a fit type of the Jewish remnant in the last days who will be faithful in the furnace of the great tribulation."

7

"THE COMING OF THE SON OF MAN"

For as the lightning cometh out of the east, and shineth even unto the west; so shall also the coming of the Son of man be. For wheresoever the carcase is, there will the eagles be gathered together. (Matt. 24:27–28)

H. A. Ironside makes an important observation about the Lord's second coming:

The coming of the Son of Man refers always to our Lord's second advent, when He will come back to the earth, in manifested glory, to set up the kingdom which the prophets foretold. This expression is never used in connection with His coming in the air for His church—a mystery still unrevealed when this discourse was given.

There are many differences between the Rapture and our Lord's second coming.

The Rapture	Christ's Revelation
The church is caught up	*The church is brought back*
"For the Lord himself shall descend from heaven with a shout, with the voice of the archangel, and with the trump of God: and the dead in Christ shall rise first: then we which are alive and remain shall be caught up together with them in the clouds, to meet the Lord in the air: and so shall we ever be with the Lord" (1 Thess. 4:16–17).	"And I saw heaven opened, and behold a white horse; and he that sat upon him was called Faithful and True, and in righteousness he doth judge and make war. And the armies which were in heaven followed him upon white horses, clothed in fine linen, white and clean" (Rev. 19:11, 14).
No unbelieving eye will see Him	*"Every eye shall see him"*
"Behold, I shew you a mystery; We shall not sleep, but we shall all be changed, in a moment, in the twinkling of an eye" (1 Cor. 15:51–52*a*).	"Behold, he cometh with clouds; and every eye shall see him" (Rev. 1:7*a*). "And then shall appear the sign of the Son of man in heaven: and then shall all the tribes of the earth mourn, and they shall see the Son of man coming in the clouds of heaven with power and great glory" (Matt. 24:30).

Christ will stop in the air	*He will return to the earth*
"Then we which are alive and remain shall be caught up together with them in the clouds, to meet the Lord in the air: and so shall we ever be with the Lord" (1 Thess. 4:17).	"And his feet shall stand in that day upon the mount of Olives, which is before Jerusalem on the east, and the mount of Olives shall cleave in the midst thereof toward the east and toward the west, and there shall be a very great valley; and half of the mountain shall remove toward the north, and half of it toward the south" (Zech. 14:4).

When Christ comes to rapture His bride, He will stop in the air; but following tribulation days, He will return to the earth to defeat the total military power of earth in the battle of Armageddon. The aftermath of that battle is recorded in Revelation 19:17–18.

> And I saw an angel standing in the sun; and he cried with a loud voice, saying to all the fowls that fly in the midst of heaven, Come and gather yourselves together unto the supper of the great God; that ye may eat the flesh of kings, and the flesh of captains, and the flesh of mighty men, and the flesh of horses, and of them that sit on them, and the flesh of all men, both free and bond, both small and great.

Verse 21 tells us, "And all the fowls were filled with their flesh." This event is what Jesus was talking about when he spoke during the Olivet Discourse of His coming: "For wheresoever the carcase is, there will the eagles be gathered together" (Matt. 24:28). In Revelation 19:17 it is called "the supper of the great God."

8

"After the Tribulation"

Immediately after the tribulation of those days shall the sun be darkened, and the moon shall not give her light, and the stars shall fall from heaven, and the powers of the heavens shall be shaken: and then shall appear the sign of the Son of man in heaven: and then shall all the tribes of the earth mourn, and they shall see the Son of man coming in the clouds of heaven with power and great glory. (Matt. 24:29–30)

Several events will take place "after the tribulation" and before Christ returns in His revelation. It is commonly accepted that on the very day the Seventieth Week comes to an end, Christ will return to the earth. That cannot be, for He declared, "But of that day and hour knoweth no man" (Matt. 24:36). That is true of the Rapture, and it is true of the Revelation.

If Christ returned on the day of the close of the Seventieth Week, then everyone could know the day. Remember, the single event that triggers that week will be the signing of a covenant to guarantee the peace of Israel for seven years (Dan. 9:27). On the day that peace treaty is signed the Seventieth Week will begin.

Since times and dates in Scripture are always related to the Jewish measurement of time with 360 days to the year, it's not difficult to determine that the seven years of Daniel 9:27 refer to a period of 2520 days.

No event announces the close of the Seventieth Week. It will simply end after 2520 days, but there will be an extension of the abomination of desolation for another thirty days. Remember, the abomination will occur in the "midst of the week" (Dan. 9:27). That means there will be 1260 days remaining in the Seventieth Week— but what about the addition of thirty days? We read of this in Daniel 12:11: "And from the time that the daily sacrifice shall be taken away, and the abomination that maketh desolate set up, there shall be a thousand two hundred and ninety days." Christ will not return during those days because when He returns there will be no worship of the Antichrist—no one will bow before his image, which is the abomination of desolation.

It should also be noted that the extension of time beyond the Seventieth Week will involve not only a thirty-day period but an additional forty-five days to bring the total period of time from the middle of the week to the millennial kingdom to 1335 days. Daniel writes, "Blessed is he that waiteth, and cometh to the thousand three hundred and five and thirty days" (Dan. 12:12).

The abomination will not only continue for thirty days past the Great Tribulation, but according to our text, "Immediately after the tribulation of those days shall the sun be darkened, and the moon shall not give her light, and the stars shall fall from heaven, and the powers of

SEVENTY-FIVE-DAY EXTENSION

RAPTURE

BEGINNING OF SORROWS	GREAT TRIBULATION	75-DAY EXTENSION	MILLENNIAL KINGDOM
1260 DAYS	1260 DAYS	30 + 45 DAYS	1,000 YEARS

← 1335 DAYS →

the heavens shall be shaken" (Matt. 24:29). It sounds like a repeat performance of the sixth seal judgment:

> And I beheld when he had opened the sixth seal, and, lo, there was a great earthquake; and the sun became black as sackcloth of hair, and the moon became as blood; and the stars of heaven fell unto the earth, even as a fig tree casteth her untimely figs, when she is shaken of a mighty wind. (Rev. 6:12–13)

One note of caution—Revelation 6:12–13 will be fulfilled during tribulation days while Matthew 24:29 will be fulfilled "immediately after the tribulation."

The next event in God's prophetic plan is found in the next verse: "And then shall appear the sign of the Son of man in heaven: and then shall all the tribes of the earth mourn, and they shall see the Son of man coming in the clouds of heaven with power and great glory" (Matt. 24:30).

It seems likely that Christ will return to the earth rather early in the final forty-five days because several judgments must take place before He sets up His kingdom and rules over the affairs of men for one thousand years. These judgments will be discussed in the remaining chapters of this book.

9

"THE FIG TREE . . . THIS GENERATION"

Now learn a parable of the fig tree; when his branch is yet tender, and putteth forth leaves, yet know that summer is nigh: so likewise ye, when ye shall see all these things, know that it is near, even at the doors. Verily I say unto you, This generation shall not pass, till all these things be fulfilled. (Matt. 24:32–34)

I have in my library many books of men who are prolific in their writings on Bible prophecy. I must say that for the most part I agree with their conclusions. I have noticed, however, that when they come to our text they have some areas of disagreement. For example, John Walvoord writes, "A common interpretation has been to interpret the fig tree as a type of Israel and the revival of Israel as the budding of the fig tree. The fig tree could very well be a type of Israel, but it does not seem to be so used in scripture . . . though many have followed this interpretation, there is no scriptural basis."[1]

Lewis Sperry Chafer agrees. "It is doubtless true that the fig tree represents in other Scriptures the nation

Israel, but there is no occasion for this meaning to be sought in the present use of that symbol."[2]

Ironside feels otherwise; he writes,

> The fig tree is the well-known symbol of Israel nationally. For many centuries the scattered Israelites, once owned by God as His own covenant people, have had no national existence. But today they are returning to Palestine in large numbers and once more indulging in the sense of again being a distinct nation. Thus the fig tree is putting forth its green leaves, and thereby proclaiming the near return of Him who is yet to be acknowledged as their Messiah and King.[3]

Concerning the term *generation*, there are also differences of opinion. John Walvoord writes,

> Jesus made a further comment on the situation in saying, "This generation will certainly not pass away until all these things have happened." . . . Some have inferred from this that the term "generation" is a reference to Israel and have asserted that Israel will not pass away until all these things are fulfilled. However, Israel will never pass away.[4]

P. B. Fitzwater has suggested, "The word 'generation' here means race, family, stock, etc., therefore it means that the Jewish race will remain intact to the end of the age."[5]

Dwight Pentecost agrees: "There has been a difference of opinion over the interpretation of 'generation' in Matthew 24:34."[6] He then lists various views that are held today and concludes with his personal preference, "others hold that the word 'generation' is to be taken in its basic usage of 'race, kindred, family, stock, breed,' so that the Lord is here promising that the nation Israel shall be preserved until the consummation of her program at the second advent in spite of the work of the Desolator to destroy her. This seems to be the best explanation."[7]

Revered scholars have differences of opinion regarding the "fig tree" and "this generation," but two truths are embraced by each of the men listed above: don't set dates and don't write off the nation of Israel.

Don't Set Dates

There are some prophecy preachers today who are enchanted with the budding of the "fig tree." They reason, "If we can determine when the nation of Israel was reborn, then we can determine the time of the end of that 'generation' and the time of Christ's return to earth in His glory."

Of course, it would be necessary to know the length of a generation. Some have concluded it is forty years; others say fifty-one years; still others say seventy years. They also disagree on the time of Israel's rebirth. Some say May 14, 1948, while others say it happened during the Six-Day War of 1967. All of this is in the interest of determining the time of our Lord's return to the earth. Some go so far as to say that once that date is discovered, all that is needed to discover the time of the rapture of the church is to back date seven years. Of course, they fail to recognize that there will be more than seven years between the Rapture and the Revelation. I believe P. B. Fitzwater was right when he wrote, "Beware of men who attempt to figure out the time of the Lord's return. Such effort dishonors God's Word, reproaches prophecy, and shipwrecks the faith of many of God's children."[8]

Allow me to again make one other observation before we leave this controversy: If the church cannot be raptured until the events of Matthew 24 take place, then the Rapture is not imminent. It is inconsistent to criticize midtribulation rapturists, prewrath rapturists, and posttribulation rapturists for their failure to believe in the imminent coming of Christ and then to declare that the church cannot be raptured today because certain events must yet be fulfilled.

Don't Write Off Israel

The most significant development of our lifetime is that the nation of Israel has been reborn. Of course, the Jew has never lost his identity, but he has had no homeland since AD 70.

There are those who would have us believe that God brought Titus and the Roman army to destroy the city of Jerusalem with its temple and to murder more than a million Jews. They believe God orchestrated the whole operation because Christ "came unto his own, and his own received him not" (John 1:11). They would have us believe that Israel's dispersion into all the world was the signal that God was through with Israel forever.

Some go so far as to say the events of Revelation happened in the first Christian century. This belief is called preterism. The preterist, according to Webster's dictionary, is "one who believes that the prophecies of the Apocalypse have already been fulfilled." John Walvoord speaks of the preterist as one who believes "the Book of Revelation is regarded as a symbolic presentation of the conflicts of the early church, making it a symbolic history of the early church rather than a prophetic revelation in the future."[9]

To the preterist I would ask, "When did Elijah and Moses witness of Christ in the days of the early church for 1260 days (Rev. 11:3)? When were they killed in the first Christian century (Rev. 11:7)? When did their bodies lie in Jerusalem for "three days and an half" (Rev. 11:9)? When did they receive new life from God and ascend up to heaven (Rev. 11:12)? And what about the 144,000, the advance of a great army of 200 million that will kill one-third of the earth's population, and a global leader who will gain control of "all kindreds, and tongues, and nations" (Rev. 7:4–8; 16:12 with 9:14–16; and 13:7)?

It is true we are now in the church age, and God is doing His work through those who make up this mystical organism, but God is not through with Israel. When the church is raptured, God, according to the book of Revelation, will pick up His dealings with Israel once again.

As we have already noted, the Antichrist will be revealed after the Rapture. He will then sign a covenant guaranteeing the right of Israel to dwell in their land in peace. The signing of that peace treaty will trigger a period of seven years (the Seventieth Week) referred to in Daniel 9:27.

In the Olivet Discourse the Lord revealed the tragic events that must take place during those seven years prior to His return to earth to set up His kingdom. Those "things," beginning with the peace initiative of the Antichrist through the end of the Great Tribulation, are the things Jesus had in mind when He said, "This generation shall not pass, till all these things be fulfilled" (Matt. 24:34).

The generation Jesus spoke of did not start in 1948 when Israel was recognized as a nation, nor did "this generation" begin during the Six-Day War of 1967. The generation Jesus referred to will be the generation that is alive during the events of the Seventieth Week. That generation will not pass till all the events of the Tribulation be fulfilled.

10

"TEN VIRGINS"

Then shall the kingdom of heaven be likened unto ten virgins, which took their lamps, and went forth to meet the bridegroom. And five of them were wise, and five were foolish. They that were foolish took their lamps, and took no oil with them: but the wise took oil in their vessels with their lamps. While the bridegroom tarried, they all slumbered and slept. And at midnight there was a cry made, Behold, the bridegroom cometh; go ye out to meet him. Then all those virgins arose, and trimmed their lamps. And the foolish said unto the wise, Give us of your oil; for our lamps are gone out. But the wise answered, saying, Not so; lest there be not enough for us and you; but go ye rather to them that sell, and buy for yourselves. And while they went to buy, the bridegroom came; and they that were ready went in with him to the marriage: and the door was shut. (Matt. 25:1–10)

We have already considered our Lord's judgment of the nations in the battle of Armageddon when "out of his mouth goeth a sharp sword, that with it he should smite the nations: and he shall rule them with a rod of iron: and he treadeth the winepress of the fierceness and wrath of Almighty God" (Rev. 19:15).

It is important to remember that the battle of Armageddon will be God's judgment of the nations—all of them. There will be another judgment spoken of as a judgment of nations, but we will come to that in the next chapter.

The judgment before us in this chapter is found in Matthew 25:1–10: "Then shall the kingdom of heaven be likened unto ten virgins."

The "virgins" of Matthew 25 refer to Jews who are still alive following Daniel's Seventieth Week and the battle of Armageddon. Dwight Pentecost writes, "There seem to be several reasons for rejecting the view that the virgins represent the church during the present age."[1] He concurs with Schuyler English, who wrote, "The ten virgins represent the remnant of Israel after the church has been taken. The five wise virgins are the believing remnant, the foolish virgins the unbelieving who only profess to be looking for Messiah's coming in power."[2] These believing and unbelieving Jews will stand before Christ in His special judgment of tribulation survivors. We read in Ezekiel 20:33–38,

> As I live, saith the Lord God, surely with a mighty hand, and with a stretched out arm, and with fury poured out, will I rule over you: and I will bring you out from the people, and will gather you out of the countries wherein ye are scattered, with a mighty hand, and with a stretched out arm, and with fury poured out. And I will bring you into the wilderness of the people, and there will I plead with you face to face. Like as I pleaded with your fathers in the wilderness of the land of Egypt, so will I plead with you, saith the Lord God. And I will cause you to pass under the rod, and I will bring you into the bond of the covenant: and I will purge out from among you the rebels, and them that transgress against me: I will bring them forth out of the country

where they sojourn, and they shall not enter into the land of Israel: and ye shall know that I am the Lord.

The believing Jews (wise virgins) will enter the kingdom still in their mortal bodies. The unbelieving Jews (foolish virgins) will be cast into hades.

Concerning this passage, John Walvoord writes,

> The annihilation of the armies that resist Christ's return will be God's judgment on the nations. After the final carnage of the Battle of Armageddon, the surviving people of the world will be judged one by one. All living Jews, the surviving nation of Israel, will be gathered from their hiding places in Palestine and throughout the world (Ezek. 39:28). Each one will face God as his judge, and none can escape this judgment. The rebels who have not accepted Christ as their Messiah prior to this second coming will be put to death (Ezek. 20:38). The rest, believing Jews who have survived the persecution of the tribulation period, will be allowed to enter the Promised Land as the first citizens of Christ's new kingdom on earth. Their hour of persecution will be finished forever, and they will receive all the blessings that have been promised to the children of Israel since the time of Abraham (see Jer. 31:31–34; Rom. 11:26–27).[3]

The statement by Paul "and so all Israel shall be saved" (Rom. 11:26) does not mean that every Jew will come to Christ. Those who survive the Tribulation and stand before Christ as "wise virgins" (believing Jews) make up the remnant of the true nation of Israel who will enter the millennial kingdom. They will enjoy the blessings promised to David for a thousand years. It will be the marriage feast (Matt. 25:10). This is not to be confused with the marriage supper of the Lamb, which is for the church and enjoyed in heaven before Christ returns to the earth (Rev. 19:7–8).

Remember, in tribulation days millions of Jews will come to Christ and trust Him as Savior, but many will reject Him. They will continue to look for their long-awaited messiah but will maintain their conviction that Jesus is not the Son of God, the true Messiah. Their thinking will resemble the belief of most Jews today—if Jesus were the true Christ, He would have ushered in the kingdom. They fail to consider the prophecy of Isaiah, who wrote these words concerning the first coming of God's Son:

> He is despised and rejected of men; a man of sorrows, and acquainted with grief: and we hid as it were our faces from him; he was despised, and we esteemed him not. Surely he hath borne our griefs, and carried our sorrows; yet we did esteem him stricken, smitten of God, and afflicted. But he was wounded for our transgressions, he was bruised for our iniquities: the chastisement of our peace was upon him; and with his stripes we are healed. All we like sheep have gone astray; we have turned every one to his own way; and the Lord hath laid on him the iniquity of us all. (Isaiah 53:3–6)

God's Son did not come the first time to set up His kingdom—He came to die for the sin of the world.

When Christ returns to earth in His second advent, He will gather together all the surviving Jews: "And he shall send his angels with a great sound of a trumpet, and they shall gather together his elect from the four winds, from one end of heaven to the other" (Matt. 24:31). As we discovered earlier, they will be taken into the wilderness (Ezek. 20:33–36). The judgment that follows will determine who are true believers (Ezek. 20:37–38).

The Scofield Reference Bible footnote of these verses in Ezekiel reads, "The passage is a prophecy of the future judgment upon Israel, regathered from all nations into the old wilderness of the wanderings (v. 35). The issue of this judgment determines who of Israel in that day shall enter the land for kingdom blessing."

The distinction between believing and unbelieving Jews is made clear in Romans 9:6, "For they are not all Israel which are of Israel." Again the Scofield footnote is an excellent commentary on this truth:

> The distinction is between Israel after the flesh, the mere natural posterity of Abraham, and Israelites who, through faith, are also Abraham's spiritual children. Gentiles who believe are also of Abraham's spiritual seed; but here the apostle is not considering them, but only the two kinds of Israelites, the natural and the spiritual Israel.

Manachim Begin, former prime minister of Israel, said, "When Messiah comes, all we have to do is ask Him, 'have you ever been here before?'" The fact is that they will know the truth then, but for the "foolish virgins" it will be too late.

11

"His Sheep . . . the Goats"

When the Son of man shall come in his glory, and all the holy angels with him, then shall he sit upon the throne of his glory: and before him shall be gathered all nations: and he shall separate them one from another, as a shepherd divideth his sheep from the goats: and he shall set the sheep on his right hand, but the goats on the left. (Matt. 25:31–33)

Scripture reveals one final judgment before the millennial kingdom begins. It is referred to in Matthew 25 as a judgment of sheep and goats. The judgment of the wise and foolish virgins will take place in the wilderness (Ezek. 20:33–38). The judgment of the sheep and the goats will be conducted in the valley of Jehoshaphat (Joel 3:2, 12).

The word *nations* is found in verse 32, but the word the Holy Spirit used when He inspired Matthew to write was the Greek word *ethnos*. From it we get our word *ethnic*. It is translated sixty-three times in the King James Bible as *nations*, but it is translated ninety-three times as *Gentiles*. The context is clear—this is not a judgment of nations as we commonly think of the term. Rather, this is a judgment of believing and unbelieving Gentiles.

"Then shall the King say unto them on his right hand, Come, ye blessed of my Father, inherit the kingdom prepared for you from the foundation of the world" (Matt. 25:34). If Christ is addressing nations, then we are to understand that everyone in a "sheep" nation will be allowed to enter the kingdom, while everyone in a "goat" nation will be doomed for all eternity. The fact is, no one is saved or lost because he is a member of some nation.

Note that the sheep (believing Gentiles) are called "righteous" in verse 37. No one is righteous before God unless he has been washed in the blood of God's Lamb. A nation cannot be washed in that precious blood. The imputed righteousness of Christ is available only to penitent sinners who open their hearts by faith and accept God's crucified and resurrected Son as Savior. Only then can a person be referred to as "His sheep" (v. 32).

Christ continues to speak to "His sheep" as He says, "For I was an hungred, and ye gave me meat: I was thirsty, and ye gave me drink: I was a stranger, and ye took me in: naked, and ye clothed me: I was sick, and ye visited me: I was in prison, and ye came unto me" (Matt. 25:35–36).

There are those who lift this text out of its context. They would have us believe that the hungry, thirsty, naked, sick, and imprisoned are people in our day who need to be helped in their present distress. Obviously, there are millions of needy people today who should be reached. It is not my intent to undermine Christ-honoring ministries to needy and suffering Jews in Israel today. Present-day believers should have a burden to help people in every station of life in order to present the gospel story to them, but the primary interpretation of Matthew 25:35–36 has do with conditions during the days of the Great Tribulation.

Remember, the Antichrist will be searching for all who have professed faith in Jesus Christ. Believing Jews will be fleeing for safety (Matt. 24:16–21). As they go, they, as well as the 144,000, will be witnessing for Jesus Christ. As we noted earlier, it will be the fulfillment of the prophecy of Matthew 24:14: "And this gospel of the kingdom shall be preached in all the world for a witness unto all nations." John records the results of this great worldwide missionary endeavor in Revelation 7:9: "After this I beheld, and, lo, a great multitude, which no man could number, of all nations, and kindreds, and people, and tongues, stood before the throne, and before the Lamb, clothed with white robes, and palms in their hands." Who are these Gentile believers? Verse 14 answers the question: "These are they which came out of great tribulation, and have washed their robes, and made them white in the blood of the Lamb." It is clear that most of those who trust Christ as Savior in tribulation days will be martyred, but many will escape.

When Jesus says to Gentile believers, "I was an hungred, and ye gave me meat: I was thirsty, and ye gave me drink: I was a stranger, and ye took me in: naked, and ye clothed me: I was sick, and ye visited me: I was in prison, and ye came unto me" (vv. 35–36), Gentile believers will respond by saying, "Lord, when saw we thee an hungred, and fed thee? or thirsty, and gave thee drink? When saw we thee a stranger, and took thee in? or naked, and clothed thee? or when saw we thee sick, or in prison, and came unto thee?" (vv. 37–39). Christ will clear the muddy waters by announcing, "Inasmuch as ye have done it unto one of the least of these my brethren, ye have done it unto me" (Matt. 25:40*b*). When Christ speaks of His "brethren," He will be referring to His national brothers—believing Jews. As these "brethren" of Jesus Christ flee into all the world, they will be proclaiming the "gospel of the kingdom" (Matt. 24:14), called the "gospel of the kingdom" because it will be preached just prior to the kingdom reign of their long-awaited Messiah. Gentiles who believe their message and trust Christ as Savior will then reach out in sympathy to their persecuted Jewish brothers. If they find a hungry Jewish believer, they will feed him. Those who are thirsty will be given drink. Strangers will be taken in. The naked will be clothed. The sick and those in prison will be visited. Gentiles will not be saved because of their loving concern for Jewish believers. No one is saved because he treats Jews with respect. The only way anyone is ever born into the family of God is through simple trust in the crucified Lamb of Calvary, but in tribulation days, one way to manifest that new life in Christ will be to tenderly care for Jewish brothers and sisters in Christ.

Unbelieving Gentiles (called goats) will manifest their rejection of Christ as Savior by their indifference and hatred toward Jewish believers.

> Then shall he say also unto them on the left hand, Depart from me, ye cursed, into everlasting fire, prepared for the devil and his angels: for I was an hungred, and ye gave me no meat: I was thirsty, and ye

gave me no drink: I was a stranger, and ye took me not in: naked and ye clothed me not: sick, and in prison, and ye visited me not. Then shall they also answer him, saying, Lord, when saw we thee an hungred, or athirst, or a stranger, or naked, or sick, or in prison, and did not minister unto thee? Then shall he answer them, saying, Verily I say unto you, Inasmuch as ye did it not to one of the least of these, ye did it not to me. And these shall go away into everlasting punishment: but the righteous into life eternal. (Matt. 25:41–46)

John Walvoord, writing on this subject, says,

A utopian world will follow the colossal failure of man's attempt to control human history. Three judgments will have purged the world of all who have not believed in Jesus Christ. The armies of the world will have been destroyed on the battlefields of the Middle East. Unbelieving Jews will have been judged and killed. In the judgment of the sheep and goats, unbelieving non-Jews will also have been purged from the earth. The entire adult population of the earth which remains will have experienced regeneration through faith in Christ.[1]

12

"Two . . . in the Field"

Then shall two be in the field; the one shall be taken, and the other left. (Matt. 24:40)

I have entitled our study *Prophecy in Context*. There is no verse that illustrates the need to leave verses in their proper setting more than Matthew 24:40.

Some well-meaning Christians have used this verse to speak of the rapture of the church, but there is nothing here regarding the Rapture. A classic verse on the Rapture is 1 Thessalonians 4:17. There we read, "Then we which are alive and remain shall be caught up together with them in the clouds, to meet the Lord in the air: and so shall we ever be with the Lord."

Notice, in the Rapture believers will be "caught up" not "taken." The logical question then is "If *taken* is not a reference to Christians who are 'caught up,' then who will be taken?" Again we look at the context,

> But as the days of Noe were, so shall also the coming of the Son of man be. For as in the days that were before the flood they were eating and drinking, marrying and giving in marriage, until the day that Noe entered into the ark, and knew not until the flood came, and took them all away; so shall also the coming of the Son of man be. (Matt. 24:37–39)

Arno Gaebelein says,

> But we return to the words of our Lord as to the days of Noah, the days when the flood came and some were taken and the others left. It has an opposite meaning. All who lived, except the house of Noah, the eight souls, were taken, swept away in judgment and those who believed and entered the ark of safety were left on earth. So will it be when the Son on Man cometh. When He returns He will find the true church no longer here. The church will be with Him. But among those on earth will be the godly remnant of Israel, awaiting His coming, also many Gentiles who turned to the Lord during the end days of the age. When the Lord returns, those who are ungodly, who refused the final call of mercy during the tribulation period, will be taken away by judgment, and those who believed the message, which God in His mercy sent forth before the return of His son, will be left on earth to enter the kingdom on earth.[1]

In the flood those who were taken away were unbelievers. Those who were left were believers, who became the first of a new generation on earth. So it will be when Christ returns to the earth in His revelation. The survivors of earth will be gathered to be judged by

Jesus Christ. The unbelievers who have come through the Great Tribulation and failed to trust Christ as Savior will be taken to hell, as were the unbelievers of Noah's day. Believers, like Noah and his family, will become the progenitors of a new race that will develop here on earth during Christ's millennial reign.

When the judgments are completed and the seventy-five-day extension comes to an end, our Lord will set up His kingdom, sit on the throne of His father David, and rule over the affairs of men for a thousand years.

Following the millennium all who are in hell will be resurrected to stand before Christ at the great white throne to be judged (Rev. 20:11–12). They will then be cast into the lake of fire, where they will experience the torments of that horrible place for eternity (Rev. 20:15). Where will you spend eternity? Will you be with the One Who became "sin for us" so that we might be "made the righteousness of God in Him" (2 Cor. 5:21)? Or will you be with Satan in that place "prepared for the devil and his angels" (Matt. 25:41)?

If you have never accepted Christ as your Savior, may I urge you to come to Him today. Believe that He took your sin upon Himself when He went to the cross and that He paid the penalty in full when He shed His blood and gave His life. As a penitent sinner, invite God's crucified and resurrected Son to enter your life. At your invitation He will come in as He promised. We read of this guarantee in Revelation 3:20, "Behold I stand at the door, and knock: if any man hear my voice, and open the door, I will come in to him." When Christ comes in, He brings life eternal, for "He that hath the Son hath life" (1 John 5:12*a*).

The next event on God's prophetic calendar is the coming of the Lord Jesus Christ to receive His bride unto Himself (1 Thess. 4:13–17; 1 Cor. 15:51–53).

This truth should produce the desire to live a Christ-like life. Consider these words from the Holy Spirit through the apostle John: "And now, little children, abide in him; that, when he shall appear, we may have confidence, and not be ashamed before him at his coming" (1 John 2:28), "and every man that hath this hope in him purifieth himself, even as he is pure" (1 John 3:3). Christians who believe in the imminent coming of Christ are careful about what they think, see, hear and say.

Finally, a Christian who is looking for Jesus will be diligent to do the work that is closest to His heart— to get the gospel into all the world. Our Lord's final commission before His ascension is still His command today: "But ye shall receive power, after that the Holy Ghost is come upon you: and ye shall be witnesses unto me both in Jerusalem, and in all Judaea, and in Samaria, and unto the uttermost part of the earth" (Acts 1:8).

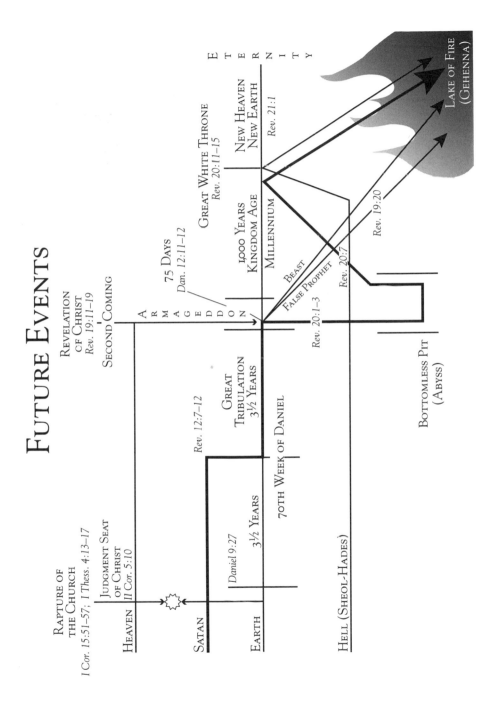

FUTURE EVENTS

RAPTURE OF THE CHURCH
1 Cor. 15:51–57; 1 Thess. 4:13–17

JUDGMENT SEAT OF CHRIST
II Cor. 5:10

REVELATION OF CHRIST
Rev. 19:11–19

SECOND COMING

75 DAYS
Dan. 12:11–12

GREAT WHITE THRONE
Rev. 20:11–15

NEW HEAVEN NEW EARTH
Rev. 21:1

ARMAGEDDON

ETERNITY

1000 YEARS KINGDOM AGE

MILLENNIUM

BEAST

FALSE PROPHET

Rev. 20:7

Rev. 20:1–3

Rev. 12:7–12

GREAT TRIBULATION 3½ YEARS

3½ YEARS

Daniel 9:27

70TH WEEK OF DANIEL

HEAVEN

SATAN

EARTH

HELL (SHEOL–HADES)

BOTTOMLESS PIT (ABYSS)

LAKE OF FIRE (GEHENNA)

Rev. 19:20

Questions and Answers

The Lord has graciously allowed me to serve Him over the past fifty-seven years as a missionary, pastor, and evangelist. Much of that ministry has been devoted to the subject of Bible prophecy. I have observed in recent years that Christians have become increasingly interested in things to come. I have received many questions from eager students of God's Word on this important subject. Some of these questions that have not been answered in this book are answered in these closing pages.

Question: **Can a person be saved in tribulation days if he rejected Christ before the Rapture?**

Answer: Second Thessalonians 2 is an important piece of God's prophetic puzzle. It tells us that before tribulation days begin the apostate church will come to its final state and Antichrist will be revealed. These two developments will precede the Seventieth Week, but they will follow the Rapture. As we discovered earlier in this book, verse 7 is referring to the restraining influence of the Holy Spirit through the church. That influence will be "taken out of the way" at the Rapture. The following verse declares,

"And then shall that Wicked [wicked one] be revealed" (2 Thess. 2:8). The "Wicked" is one of twenty-six names or titles of the Antichrist. The order of events is clear—the Rapture will occur, and then the Antichrist will "be revealed." Remember, the Seventieth Week does not begin at the time of the Rapture. It will begin when the Antichrist signs the covenant guaranteeing the peace of Israel for seven years. (Dan. 9:27) This is a strong argument for a pretribulation rapture. When the Seventieth Week begins, the church will be gone.

It is my conviction that the following verses answer this question of whether someone can be saved after the Rapture if he rejected Christ before. "And with all deceivableness of unrighteousness in them that perish; because they received not the love of the truth, that they might be saved. And for this cause God shall send them strong delusion, that they should believe a lie: that they all might be damned who believed not the truth, but had pleasure in unrighteousness" (2 Thess. 2:10–12).

Ironside had this to say on this subject: "I have run across the error in many recent books on the coming of the Lord. That after the rapture of the church there will be a great revival, and unprecedented spiritual awakening in Christendom, when a vast number of people who have been undecided during the present dispensation of grace will turn to the Lord; and it is being widely taught that these will form the great multitude of Gentiles who will be saved out of the tribulation. Let me say, I have searched my Bible diligently for any confirmation of such teaching, but I fail to find it. On the contrary, we are distinctly told in 2 Thessalonians 2:11 that God is going to give up those who during this present age receive not the love of the truth that they might be saved; they will be given up to hardness of heart and perversity of spirit."[1]

Dr. Lehman Strauss agrees: "Those who deliberately reject the love of the truth in this age are without hope in the coming age."[2]

Question: **What happens to martyred tribulation saints?**

Answer: Millions of people will come to Christ during tribulation days. Some of them will "endure unto the end" (Matt. 24:13), but a great multitude will be martyred (Rev. 7:9–14). The same promise that applies to Christians who die in this age of grace will certainly apply to believers who are martyred in tribulation days: "We are confident, I say, and willing rather to be absent from the body, and to be present with the Lord" (2 Cor. 5:8).

Three kinds of bodies are mentioned in Scripture: "There are also celestial bodies, and bodies terrestrial: but the glory of the celestial is one, and the glory of the terrestrial is another. There is one glory of the sun, and another glory of the moon, and another glory of the stars: for one star differeth from another star in glory. So also is the resurrection of the dead. It is sown in corruption; it is raised in incorruption" (1 Cor. 15:40–42).

The three kinds of bodies are: terrestrial (natural) bodies, celestial (heavenly) bodies, and incorruptible (glorified) bodies. Tribulation saints, like believers today, will walk this earth in their natural bodies. When they die, they will be clothed with their temporary celestial bodies. They, like all believers, will be resurrected in (glorified) bodies.

The apostle John speaks of this in Revelation 20:4–5: "And I saw thrones, and they sat upon them, and judgment was given unto them: and I saw the souls of them that were beheaded for the witness of Jesus, and for the word of God, and which had not worshipped the beast, neither his image, neither had received his mark upon their foreheads, or in their hands; and they lived and reigned with Christ a thousand years. . . . This is the first resurrection."

Question: **Will Old Testament saints receive glorified bodies at the time of the Rapture?**

Answer: There is a difference of opinion on this question among godly commentators, but I believe that the rapture of the church is the rapture of the *church.* If we consider Old Testament saints to be a part of the church, we create more questions than could ever be answered.

For example, Elijah and Moses will be killed in the middle of the Seventieth Week. If these Old Testament saints received glorified bodies at the time of the Rapture, how could they die in the days of tribulation?

Old Testament saints are in heaven with their celestial bodies, but they will not receive glorified bodies until Christ returns to the earth in His revelation—perhaps at the same time martyred tribulation saints receive their glorified bodies.

Job declared, "And though after my skin worms destroy this body, yet in my flesh shall I see God" (Job 19:26). Our question to Job is "When will such a miracle take place?" His answer is found in verse 25, "For I know that my redeemer liveth, and that he shall stand at the latter day upon the earth."

Question: **What is the first resurrection?**

Answer: The first resurrection is in several stages. In Matthew 27:52–53 we read, "And the graves were opened; and many bodies of the saints which slept arose, and came out of the graves after his resurrection, and went into the holy city, and appeared unto many." The Scofield Reference Bible footnote for this passage is helpful. "That these bodies returned to their graves is not said and may not be inferred. The wave-sheaf typifies the resurrection of Christ, but a sheaf implies plurality. It was a single 'corn of wheat' that fell into the ground in the crucifixion and entombment of Christ (John 12:24); it was a sheaf which came forth in resurrection. The inference is that these saints, with the spirits of 'just men made perfect' (Heb. 12:23) from Paradise, went with Jesus (Eph. 4:8–10) into heaven."

If those who came out of the graves after our Lord's resurrection received glorified bodies, then they would be a part of the first resurrection.

The next stage of the first resurrection will take place at the Rapture. "Behold, I shew you a mystery; we shall not all sleep, but we shall all be changed, in a moment, in the twinkling of an eye, at the last trump: for the trumpet shall sound, and the dead shall be raised incorruptible, and we shall be changed. For this corruptible must put on incorruption, and this mortal must put on immortality" (1 Cor. 15:51–53). First Thessalonians 4:16 declares, "For the Lord himself shall descend from heaven with a shout, with the voice of the archangel, and with the trump of God: and the dead in Christ shall rise first."

In Revelation 11 we have the account of the witness and the death of Elijah and Moses. In the middle of the Seventieth Week a spectacular event will take place: "The Spirit of life from God entered into them, and they stood upon their feet; and great fear fell upon them which saw them. And they heard a great voice from heaven saying unto them, Come up hither. And they ascended up to heaven in a cloud; and their enemies beheld them" (Rev. 11:11–12). It is inferred that Elijah and Moses will receive their glorified bodies and be raptured to meet their blessed Lord. This part of the first resurrection will involve only two men.

As we noted earlier, Old Testament saints will receive their glorified bodies when Christ returns to the earth (Job 19:25).

Question: **Will the church be a part of Christ's kingdom reign?**

Answer: It is important to understand that David will be Christ's regent governing the nation of Israel in our Lord's millennial kingdom.

Hosea 3:5 declares, "Afterward shall the children of Israel return, and seek the Lord their God, and David their king; and shall fear the Lord and his goodness in the latter days." We read further in Ezekiel 34:23–24, "And I will set up one shepherd over them, and he shall feed them, even my servant David; he shall feed them, and he shall be their shepherd. And I the Lord will be their God, and my servant David a prince among them; I the Lord have spoken it."

The twelve apostles will judge the twelve tribes of Israel. God promised, "I will restore thy judges as at the first" (Isa. 1:26*a*). Speaking to His apostles, Jesus said, "Verily I say unto you, That ye which have followed me, in the regeneration when the Son of man shall sit in the throne of his glory, ye also shall sit upon twelve thrones, judging the twelve tribes of Israel" (Matt. 19:28).

Keeping in mind that the rapture of the church will be part of the first resurrection, consider Revelation 20:6, "Blessed and holy is he that hath part in the first resurrection: on such the second death hath no power, but they shall be priests of God and of Christ, and shall reign with him a thousand years." It was to the church Paul wrote, "Do ye not know that the saints shall judge the world?" (1 Cor. 6:2*a*).

David will be governing the nation of Israel, the twelve apostles will be judging the twelve tribes, the church will be involved in reigning with Christ, but, best of all, Christ will be on the throne of His father David ruling over Israel and all the world.

You may find it helpful to read a companion volume I have written entitled *God's Prophetic Blueprint*, also published by BJU Press.

ENDNOTES

Chapter 1

1. Harold Camping, *1994?* (New York: Vantage Press, 1992), 458.
2. Edgar C. Whisenant, *The Rapture: Rosh Hash Ana, 1988, and 88 Reasons Why* (Edgar C. Whisenant, 1987).
3. Edgar Whisenant and Greg Brewer, *The Final Shout: Rapture Report 1989* (World Bible Society, 1989).

Chapter 2

1. For a timetable of events see John H. Kerr, *A Harmony of the Gospels* (Grand Rapids: Fleming H. Revell, 1903, 1924), xvi, xvii.
2. John F. Walvoord and Roy B. Zuck, *The Bible Knowledge Commentary* (Wheaton: Victor Books, 1983), 76.

Chapter 3

1. J. Dwight Pentecost, *Things to Come* (Grand Rapids: Zondervan Publishing House, 1964), 204.
2. H. A. Ironside, *Daniel* (Neptune, NJ: Loizeaux Brothers, 1911), 137.

Chapter 5

1. J. Dwight Pentecost, *Things to Come* (Grand Rapids: Zondervan Publishing House, 1964), 205.

2. Pentecost, 271.

Chapter 7

1. H. A. Ironside, *Notes on Matthew* (Neptune, NJ: Loizeaux Brothers, 1948), 337.

Chapter 9

1. John F. Walvoord, *The Prophecy Knowledge Handbook* (Wheaton: Victor Books, 1990), 390–91.
2. Lewis Sperry Chafer, quoted in Pentecost, *Things to Come*, 281.
3. H. A. Ironside, *Notes on Matthew* (Neptune, NJ: Loizeaux Brothers, 1948), 323.
4. John F. Walvoord, *The Prophecy Knowledge Handbook* (Wheaton: Victor Books, 1990), 391.
5. P. B. Fitzwater, *Preaching and Teaching the New Testament*, (Chicago: Moody Press, 1957), 86
6. J. Dwight Pentecost, *Things to Come* (Grand Rapids: Zondervan Publishing House, 1964), 281.
7. Pentecost, 281
8. P. B. Fitzwater, *Preaching and Teaching the New Testament* (Chicago: Moody Press, 1957), 86.
9. John F. Walvoord, *The Prophecy Knowledge Handbook* (Wheaton: Victor Books, 1990), 519.

Chapter 10

1. J. Dwight Pentecost, *Things to Come* (Grand Rapids: Zondervan Publishing House, 1964), 283.
2. Schuyler English, *Studies in the Gospel According to Matthew*, quoted in Pentecost, *Things to Come*, 283.
3. John F. Walvoord with John E. Walvoord, *Armageddon* (Grand Rapids: Zondervan Publishing House, 1974), 177–78.

Chapter 11

1. Walvoord, 179.

Chapter 12

1. Arno Clemens Gaebelein, *As It Was—So Shall It Be* (Publication Office, Our Hope, 1937), 92

Questions and Answers

1. H. A. Ironside, *Lectures on the Revelation* (Neptune, NJ: Loizeaux Brothers, 1920), 133–34.
2. Lehman Strauss, *The Book of the Revelation* (Neptune, NJ: Loizeaux Brothers, 1964), 175.